BORSTAL BOY
A
PUNK ROCK OPERA

A true story put to music designed to be performed in prisons.

David Clarke

Published By Bierton Particular Baptists
11 Hayling Close
Fareham
Hampshire
PO143AE

ISBN 978-1-4709-8526-4

Publication Date: 11 February 2014
Yet to be performed in prisons

THE STORY (Publishers note)

This Opera is intended to be performed by a live Punk Rock Band.

Endorsement

Rebecca Porter <rebeccastephanieporter@gmail.com>

To
info@pimlicoopera.co.uk
CC

20 Apr 2014

Whom it May Concern;

Borstal Boy Punk Opera

My producer will be contacting you with a working libretto for consideration. It's called "Borstal Boy'; and is a mature piece of work at an advanced stage of editing/rewriting. It would fit well within the ethos of the Pimlico Opera Company, as it concerns redemption within a prison setting.

This project is ready to be revised for staging, with a view to touring prisons, and is a original piece inspired by the early life of my producer. It's the story of a bad lad made good.

The Libretto

My involvement with the project has been limited to writing the libretto; which the author owns, as it is his life story. I am hopeful that this project will be staged, as it is a brilliant tale.

Yours sincerely,

Rebecca Porter

YouTube Playlist Borstal Boy Punk Rock Opera

Contents

David Clarke	1
THE STORY (Publishers note)	3
This Opera is intended to be performed with a live Punk Rock Band.	3
Endorsement	3
BORSTAL BOY-CALL SHEET	6
BORSTAL BOYS-CAST	10
A PUNK ROCK OPERA	11
ACT ONE	12
SCENE ONE: GRAFFITI WALL	12
SCENE ONE: WALL SCENE (CONTINUED)	13
SCENE ONE DAVE AND MICK	15
SCENE TWO: SATURDAY NIGHT DANCE HIGH SCHOOL	20
Click To View On Youtube	20
SCENE THREE: CHIP SHOP SCENE	26
SCENE THREE: CHIP SHOP SCENE (Continued)	32
SCENE FOUR: BEDROOM SCENE	35
SCENE FIVE: PUB SCENE	40
ACT TWO	47
SCENE SIX: PRISON CELL AT DOVER BORSTAL	47
SCENE SEVEN: PRISON RELEASE	56
SCENE EIGHT: BEDROOM	60
SCENE NINE: COURT ROOM	67
SCENE TEN: PUB	73
SCENE ELEVEN: PUB SCENE Continued	76
FURTHER PUBLICATIONS	
CONVERTED ON LSD TRIP	82
BORSTAL BOYS	83
BORSTAL BOYS PUNK ROCK OPERA	84
AND SUCH WERE SOME OF YOU	85
AND SUCH WERE SOME OF YOU	86
TROJAN WARRIORS	86
BEFORE THE COCK CROWS PART 1, 2 AND 3.	88
THE FALL, DESPERATION AND RECOVERY	89

BORSTAL BOY-CALL SHEET
ACT ONE

SCENE ONE: GRAFFITI

SONG INTRO- GOD SAVE THE QUEEN
The Sex Pistols

1. Master of ceremonies (Narrator)
2. Cast of performers
3. Bad influences

SCENE ONE: WALL SCENE (CONTINUED)

SONG ONE – COMPLETE CONTROL
The Clash

SCENE TWO: SATURDAY NIGHT DANCE GIRLS HIGH SCHOOL

SCENE TWO-TEENAGE KICKS
The Undertones

SONG THREE – NEW ROSE
The Damned

SONG FOUR-LOVE SONG
The Damned

SONG FIVE-EVER FALLEN IN LOVE
Buzzcocks

SCENE THREE: CHIP SHOP SCENE (Sue and her High School Girls)

1. Sue and her High School girls
2. Dave is popular with her friends including his band "**The Fowler Mean**"

SCENE FOUR: CHIP SHOP SCENE (Dave's Dodgy Mates))

SONG SIX – JILTED JOHN

Jilted John

SONG SEVEN - DID YOU NO WRONG
Sex Pistols

1. Narrator summarises the break-up
2. Dave gets in on the argument
3. Everyone has an opinion.

SCENE FIVE: BEDROOM SCENE Dave shows his feelings for Sue

SONG EIGHT – STRANGLEHOLD
UK Subs

SCENE SIX: PUB SCENE

SONG NINE – STARING AT THE RUDE BOYS
The Rutts

SONG TEN - A BOMB
The Jam

SONG ELEVEN – I'M AN UPSTART
Angelic Upstarts

SONG TWELVE - WHITE RIOT
The Clash

1. Webley Air Pistol
2. The Fight scene

ACT TWO

SCENE SEVEN: PRISON CELL AT DOVER BORSTAL

SONG THIRTEEN - THE WAIT
Killing Joke

SONG FOURTEEN - I COULDN'T BE YOU
UK Subs

1. God and the Devil visit Dave in his prison cell

SONG FIFTEEN I FOUGHT THE LAW

The Clash
SCENE EIGHT: PUB SCENE Dave released from Borstal

SONG SIXTEEN -READY STEADY GO
Generation X
SCENE NINE: BEDROOM

SONG SEVENTEEN-NICE AND SLEAZY
Stranglers
1. God challenged by the Devil and accuses Dave .

SONG EIGHTEEN- PRETTY VACANT
Sex Pistols

1. Dave is going to take acid.
2. Trippy scene

SONG NINETEEN- CAPTAIN KIRK
Spizzenergi

SCENE TEN: COURT ROOM
1. Dave tries to explain why he is confessing

SONG TWENTY- SOMETHING THAT I SAID
The Rutts
2. Dave explains crime is a state of mind

SONG TWENTY ONE-BORSTAL BREAKOUT
Sham 69
3. Court Bestows Sentence Dave predicts his difficult future.

SONG TWENTY TWO-SHOULD I STAY OR SHOULD I GO
The Clash

SCENE ELEVEN: PUB Continued
1 Master of ceremonies summarizes

SONG TWENTY THREE -FEELIN' ALRIGHT WITH THE CREW
999

SONG TWENTY-FOUR-POLICE AND THIEVES
The Clash

Uplifting final message (all cast do a bit)

SONG TWENTY FIVE: MR VERY GUILTY
The Borstal boys

Key:

Typeface	**Meaning**
UNDERLINED	Act One or Act Two
BOLD	Dramatic Scene
1. Plain text	Content of Dramatic Scene
	Spoken or Sung/Delivered as performer Requests
ITALICS	Songs for the 'The Band'
Highlighted Text	Suggested stage directions

BORSTAL BOYS-CAST

Dave Clarke - Bad lad turned good
Dave's brother Mick Clarke- Bad Lad in control
Sue Girl Friend
Sue's Friends (3)
God (Magistrate and Chairman)
The Devil (Magistrate)
Magistrate
Press
Court Official
Master of Ceremonies/The Narrator
Landlord
Chip Shop Owner

BORSTAL BOYS-EXTRAS
Policemen (several)
MOD Crowd (several)
Dave's Mate 1
Dave's mate 2
Rocker Crowd several
Dave's Mates Gang
Dave's Mates new friends
Villain Firm
Villain Firm leader 1
Bikers
Biker 1
Biker Girl

BORSTAL BOY
A PUNK ROCK OPERA

MUSICAL DIRECTOR

MUSICIANS

STORY BORSTAL BOY

Libretto
REBECCA PORTER

Trojan Horse International presents Borstal Boy a Punk Opera. Designed to be performed in prisons.

This opera is based on the true story as told in the book Borstal Boys for prison inmates.

ACT ONE

Click to View on Youtube
SCENE ONE: GRAFFITI WALL

Direction

The main curtain opens showing only a brick wall
Two Police man are Standing Left and Right starring into space
(Dave) creeps behind the coppers and sprays Borstal Boy, then title of the opera, on the Wall.
As the Coppers turn and notice Dave they call out but Dave runs rings around them as they are moving at half pace and cannot catch him.

Cast Required
Dave
Copper 1
Copper 2
Action

13

Coppers notice Dave spraying and say:

[Copper 1]:

"Oi !! Lad what do you think your up to ?" !!!

[Dave]: says sarcastically

"Its Art Mat"
(Sarcastically)

[Copper 2]:

Oh come back here !

Action
And gets chased off.

SCENE ONE: WALL SCENE (CONTINUED)

Direction

The Narrator introduces the story and he is like a Demented Circus Ring Master and Speaks From a Pulpit
Mick bullies Dave and is soon arrested and carted off by the police and sent to Borstal.
Scene to establish Mick as Dave's brother as a bully in total control

influencing Dave to his every whim.

Cast Required

Dave
Mick (Dave's Brother)
Copper 1
Copper 2
Narrator

Action
[Narrator]:

"Ladies and Gentleman Welcome to This Festival Of Anarchy?"

"The International Production Company Trojan Horse proudly present to you "Borstal Boy." It tells of the trials and tribulations of a roustabout rescapalion revolutionary by the name of Dave Clarke. Its his story, a tale of misfortune and wealth, of love, love turned sour and through influence and bad choices a life of petty crime and the events that turned his life around.

Our story, like all the best stories, comes with music, music performed by:

SONG INTRODUCTION: GOD SAVE THE QUEEN
The Queen Sex Pistols
God save the queen
The fascist regime
They made you a moron
A potential H bomb
God save the queen
She's not a human being
and There's no future
And England's dreaming
Don't be told what you want
Don't be told what you need
There's no future
No future
No future for you

They will help and guide us across this murky river.

15

Watch out for the gruesome cast of horrors that make up our players this evening. Most of them are bad characters, the like of which you would cross the street to avoid. Allow me to introduce to you to you one that is possibly the worst. He is David's elder brother Mick, a role model with no compassion nor responsibility and he is in complete control of Dave".

Dave runs on the stage and meets Mick who is now in centre stage.

Direction:
Mike Clarke and Dave Clarke are on stage. Dave Clarke is listening to Mike Clarke, but hardly with rapt attention.

SCENE ONE DAVE AND MICK

Dave and Mick

[Mike Clarke]:

What have you been up to running from the police ?

[Dave Clarke]:

On the spay can you know I like my fun.

[Mike Clarke]:

Now don't be so stupid and don't take stupid risks

[Dave Clarke]:

It's only a bit of fun

[Mike Clarke]:

You know we've got it good, thieving and dealing so don't do things to mess it up. So listen here, little brother, let me explain how things need to happen. You wanna be a legend like me, you need to listen.

[Dave Clarke]:

Listen? But I'm not so sure about stealing...just for the sake of it. Yeah I nicked a few bits and pieces, but I needed them for the band....

[Mike Clarke]:

You told me you had no conscience about nicking that amplifier from the Catholic Church so whats all the fuss about.

[Dave Clarke]:

Well I needed that amp for my guitar and besides I remeber mum talling me, when we were young, the Catholics were wrong anyway so I did let that bother me.

[Mike Clarke]:

You never minded me giving you that motor bike (150 CC Francis Barnet Motor bike) that I nicked from the College, did yeh.

[Dave Clarke]:

No but that was you and I didn't know who it belelonged too any way so I didn't let that bother me.

[Mike Clarke]:
Well that how things are so stop being such a cissy. No brother of mine is

going to be a fanny about doing a bit of robbing....

[Dave Clarke]:

Yeah, alright....I mean I suppose it's not too bad.

[Mike Clarke]:

Maybe dealing with a few piles, a bit of blow....selling drugs to rich kids. Who gets hurt doing that...?

[Dave Clarke]:

....yeah. I guess. I mean.....

[Mike Clarke]:

And then after that I'll show you how to shake people down for money. 'Protection money', we call that....

[Dave Clarke]:

Oh yeah? Protection from other lads like us...?

[Mike Clarke]:

Yeah and if you don't do exactly as I say then you'll need protection. But there'll be no other geezer around to offer it, so you'll just have to clear out of town.

[Dave Clarke]:

Nah that's alright. I'll be alright.

[Mike Clarke]:

Yeah I got the wheels and I got the reputation, and I'll teach you about how to be bad. Don't you forget I got 'Complete Control' over you...

Direction:

18

As The Band play 'Complete Control' Mike is arrested and taken away leaving his scooter on stage next to Dave.

Action

Coppers appear and after a scuffle arrest Mick.
Dave gets away.

[Copper 1]:

"We've been looking for you Mick.

[Copper 2]:

"Yeah nice little bonus for us finding you, we'll deal with your brother another time".
Action

Dave now Address' the audience while cuffs go on Mick.

[Dave]:

"This is not good, my brothers got nicked. I need him. He keeps me on the straight and narrow. I love him. I'd do any thing for him. For some reason he likes **Complete Control.**

<u>SONG ONE –COMPLETE CONTROL</u>
The Clash

They said release 'Remote Control'
But we didn't want it on the label
They said, "Fly to Amsterdam"
The people laughed but the press went mad

Ooh ooh ooh someone's really smart
Ooh ooh ooh complete control, that's a laugh

On the last tour my mates couldn't get in
I'd open up the back door but they'd get run out again

At every hotel we was met by the Law
Come for the party - come to make sure!

Ooh ooh ooh have we done something wrong?
Ooh ooh ooh complete control, even over this song

They said we'd be artistically free
When we signed that bit of paper
They meant let's make a lotsa mon-ee
An' worry about it later

Ooh ooh ooh I'll never understand
Ooh ooh ooh complete control - lemme see your other hand!

All over the news spread fast
They're dirty, they're filthy
They ain't gonna last!

This is Joe Public speaking
I'm controlled in the body, controlled in the mind

Total
C-o-n control - that means you!

[Narrator]:

Wrong place at the wrong time for old mike he got it bad, arrested and charged with stealing cars. He was found guilty and got sent down to Rochester Borstal..

End of Scene One

SCENE TWO: SATURDAY NIGHT DANCE HIGH SCHOOL
Click To View On Youtube

Direction

In this scene Dave with his mates gate crash Aylesbury Girls High School Dance.
Sue and her mates are there.
Everyone is there on stage

[Narrator]:

We now meet Dave left to his own devices . His first plan was to get some action at the local girls school dance.

Action
Dave with mates

[Dave Mate 1]:

"That's your brothers scooter isn't it Dave?"

[Dave]:

"Yeah he doesn't need it any more
Dave Mate 2 We remember brother coming up town on it when he got ride of his motor bike. He loved his scooter he spayed it metalic blue and had fire covered dual seat and a back rest.

Dave Mate 1 Yeh we all thought Mike was good fun we used to have

good time together.
[Dave Mate 2]:

"Do you reckon we'll get into the school dance ?"

[Dave]:

"No problem lets have some fun".

Action

Sue with her Mates

[Sue's best mate JANET 1]:

"Hey Sue check out those boys".

[Sue]:

"Oh yes the one on the scooter looks nice".

Action:
Dave Clarke and his Mates leave the scooter and cross the stage to the girls. They still hang back a bit though. They pretend not to hear the girls

[Sue's best mate JANET 1]:

Who are those boys over there? One came here on a scooter...I heard it...

[Sue's mate lucy 2]:

That is so amazing. He looks so cool. I bet he's not even in school anymore.

[Sue's mate Sally 3]:

I wonder what he does all day...? Do you think he has a job or something.

[Sue]:

I don't know. He is handsome.

[Sue's Best Mate JANET 1]:

Is he looking at you? I think he's looking at me. Maybe he's looking at Lucy...?

[Sue's mate Lucy 2]:

No I think he likes Sue. He's looking at Silver Sue.

[Sue's mate Sally 3]:

Well he's all the way over there and we're over here, so who cares who he's looking at if he's too afraid to come and talk to us...?

[Dave Clarke]: //SPEAKING TO HIS MATES

Right lads there's plenty here, we'll get some tonight.

[Dave's Mates]:

Yeah man and once we tell these girls about your reputation....

[Dave]:

I have the best worst reputation.

[Dave's Mates]:

...and when we tell them about your brother in Borstal....

[Dave]:

Yeah all the good girls like a bit of a bad boy...

Direction
Every body Dancing

SONG TWO- TEENAGE KICKS

Undertones

A teenage dream's so hard to beat
Every time she walks down the street
Another girl in the neighbourhood
Wish she was mine, she looks so good
I wanna hold her, wanna hold her tight
Get teenage kicks right through the night
I'm gonna call her on the telephone
Have her over cos I'm all alone
I need excitement, oh I need it bad
And it's the best I've ever had
I wanna hold her, wanna hold her tight
Get teenage kicks right through the night
Alright
A teenage dream's so hard to beat
Every time she walks down the street
Another girl in the neighbourhood
Wish she was mine, she looks so good
I wanna hold her, wanna hold her tight
Get teenage kicks right through the night
I'm gonna call her on the telephone
Have her over cos I'm all alone
I need excitement, oh I need it bad
And it's the best I've ever had
I wanna hold her, wanna hold her tight
Get teenage kicks right through the night
Alright
I wanna hold her, wanna hold her tight
Get teenage kicks right through the night
Alright

Direction

Dave Clarke and Silver Sue are dancing together. SUE'S FRIENDS (JANET), LUCY, SALLY) are in a group together, they are shaking their heads, pointing and laughing at David Clarke and Silver Sue.

<u>SONG THREE –NEW ROSE</u>
The Damned

Is she realy going out with him ?
Ah!
I gotta a feelin' inside of me
It's kinda strange like a stormy sea
I don't know why, I don't know why
I guess these things have gotta be
I gotta new rose, I got her good
Guess I knew that I always would
I can't stop to mess around
Like a brand new rose in town
See the sun, see the sun it shines
Don't get too close or it'll burn your eyes
Don't you run away that way
You can come back another day

I never thought this could happen to me
I feel so strange, so why should it be
I don't deserve somebody this great
I'd better go or it'll be too late, yeah
Ah!

Action

During the next song Dave serenades Sue with hand on heart to Love Song.

SONG FOUR-LOVE SONG
The Damned

I'll be the ticket if you're my collector

I've got the fare if you're my inspector

I'll be the luggage, if you'll be the porter

I'll be the parcel if you'll be my sorter

(chorus)

Just for you here's a love song

Just for you here's a love song

And it makes me glad to say

It's been a lovely day

And it's okay

I'll be the mail, you'll be the guard

I'll be the ink on your season ticket card

I'll be the rubbish, you'll be the bin
I'll be the paint on the sign if you'll be the tin
(chorus)
(chorus)

Its Okay

Its Okay

[Narrator]:

Ah our poor, poor Dave Clarke has followed his...Instincts...and reckons he's found true love. Shame all his thievery is about to ruin things.... these relationships can go wrong very quickly.

End Of Scene Two

SCENE THREE: CHIP SHOP SCENE

Direction

Dave and Sue Have an argument and she steam's off.
She's possibly pregnant but feels better off without Dave.
Her 3 mates taunt and tease Dave (they want to get off with Dave)
He gets found out by Sue and she dumps Him
Dave and his mates are with him
Dave chats to his mates about Sue, slagging her off, putting on a brave face
The Chip Shop owner gives Dave Clarke some free chips, and has the till robbed for her kindness.

Cast Required

Dave
Dave's Mates
Sue
Sue's 3 Friends
Narrator
Chip Shop Owner

[Narrator]:

Three months have passed and Dave's life style of petty crime, stupid kicks and sculduggery were pissing Sue right off !
We now catch up with Dave and his mates then Sue and her mates at the

local Chip Shop. Dave and Mates turn up at the chip shop

[Dave's Mate 1]:

"What's Up Dave, Mate you're looking a bit down?"

[Dave]:

"I think Sue might be up the pregnant"

[Dave Mate 1]:

"Woah what are you going to do ?"

[Dave]:

" Come on lads you know I've got no time for that" (laughs)

Action

Sues Mates arrive at the chip shop and start talking to each other.
Sue's comes into the Chip Shop and ignores Dave Clarke/DAVE'S MATES.

[Sues best mate Janet 1]:

Seriously what do Sue do you see in this fool?

[Sue's mate Lucy]:

Well it was fun, he was fun....

[Sues best mate Janet 1]:

He's such a loser. A loser. Awful. You know he's got no job...

[Sues's mate Sally 3]:

...no future...

[Sues's best mate Janet 1]:

...but he does have a cool scooter....

[Sue]:

What the hell is this rubbish! He's not cool, he's a loser...

[Sue's best mate Janet 1]:

> Oh, THAT boy, that's the one we want
> He's so smart, he's the cutest one
> But, Oh, no job where's his money from?
> (2 times)

[Sue mate Lucy 2]:

> He's bad, he's bad, he's baaad
> Oh, THAT Sue, we could pull her hair

[Sue mate Sally 3]:

> She's with our man, we'll just glare
> We'd do anything, just any thing
> To be the only girl for him

[All three Sues's Mates 1, 2 and 3]:

> Oh, THAT boy, that's the one we want
> He's so smart, he's the cutest one
> But, Oh, no job where's his money from? (2 times)
> He's bad, he's bad, he's baaad

Action

Dave and Sue talking

[Dave]:

Hey baby I've been waiting for you. Wants some chips

What's wrong Sue, you're not listening to them

[Sue]:

No Thanks. What have you been doing all day ?

[Dave]:

Why you gotta be like that, Sue ? You know I'm not a nine to fiver. You know our love does not need money.. or anything like that.

[Sue]:

Oh I see now I understand
Now I get why we don't need a plan
you'll steal and lie and steal some more
There's no need for a job we'll steal food from the store.

Thanl God I'm not pregnant
I won't be stuck with a losser like you any more
You are so dumped

[Dave]:

Ever fallen in Love with someone you shouldn't have

Action

Sue gets consoled by her mates .
Dave is shaking his head in confusion.
His mates congratulate him on his new found freedom.

SONG FIVE-EVER FALLEN IN LOVE

Buzzcocks

You spurn my natural emotions
You make me feel like dirt
And i'm hurt
And if i start a commotion
I run the risk of losing you
And that's worse

Ever fallen in love with someone
Ever fallen in love
In love with someone
Ever fallen in love
In love with someone
You shouldn't've fallen in love with

I can't see much of a future
Unless we find out what's to blame
What a shame
And we won't be together much longer
Unless we realize that we are the same

Ever fallen in love with someone
Ever fallen in love
In love with someone
Ever fallen in love
In love with someone
You shouldn't've fallen in love with

You disturb my natural emotions
You make me feel like dirt
And i'm hurt
And if i start a commotion
I'll only end up losing you
And that's worse

Ever fallen in love with someone
Ever fallen in love
In love with someone
Ever fallen in love
In love with someone
You shouldn't've fallen in love with

Ever fallen in love with someone
Ever fallen in love
In love with someone
Ever fallen in love
In love with someone

You shouldn't've fallen in love with
Fallen in love with
Ever fallen in love with someone
You shouldn't've fallen in love with

END OF SCENE THREE
SCENE THREE: CHIP SHOP SCENE (Continued)

Action
Dave enters the chip shop
Girls and Boys exit stage area. Leaving Dave at the chip shop

[Chip Ship Shop Owner]

"Are you OK Love?"

[Dave]:

"Not really my girl friend has just dumped me".

[Chip Shop Owner]:

"Never mind sweetheart here you can have some chips free on the house".

[Dave]:

"Thanks that's really nice".

[Chip shop owner]:

"No problem ..... there's plenty more fish in the sea".

Action

Chip shop owner leaves the shop to get more fish.
Dave nicks the till and runs off
Chip Shop Owner rushes back in the shop.

[Chip Shop Owner]:

"Oi! get back here you thieving little sod.

[Dave]:

Well I'm a jilted John now you know what its like to suffer.

Action

Dave joins the band to sing Jilted John.

SONG SIX – JILTED JOHN
Jilted John

I've been going out with a girl,
her name is Julie
But last night she said to me,
when we were watching telly
(This is what she said)
She said listen John, I love you
But there's this bloke, I fancy
I don't want to two time you,
so it's the end for you and me
Who's this bloke I asked her
Goooooordon, she replied
Not THAT puff, I said dismayed
Yes but he's no puff she cried
(He's more of a man than you'll ever be)
Here we go, two three four
I was so upset that I cried,

all the way to the chip shop
When I came out there was Gordon,
standing at the bus stop
(And guess who was with him? Yeah, Julie, and they were both laughing at me)
Oh, she is cruel and heartless
to pack me for Gordon
Just cos he's better looking than me
Just cos he's cool and trendy
But I know he's a moron, Gordon is a moron
Gordon is a moron, Gordon is a moron
Here we go, two three four
Oh she's a slag and he's a creep
She's a tart, he's very cheap
She is a slut, he thinks he's tough
She is a bitch, he is a puff
Yeah yeah, it's not fair
Yeah yeah, it's not fair
(I'm so upset)
I'm so upset, I'm so upset, yeah yeah
(I ought to smash his face in.)
(Yeah, but he's bigger than me. In't he?)
(I know, I'll get my mate Barry to hit him. He'd flatten him)
(Yeah but Barry's a mate of Gordon's in'e?)
(Oh well, I don't care)
I don't care
I don't care
Cause she's a slag and he's a creep
she's a tart, he's very cheap
she is a slut, he thinks he's tough......

End Of Scene Three

SCENE FOUR: BEDROOM SCENE

Direction

    Narrator slags off Dave
    Dave reflects
    Dave redeems himself to the audience
    Confesses his true feelings for Sue. She has a strangle hold on him.

Cast Required

Dave
Mick
Narrator

Action

    Narrator slags of f Dave

[Narrator]:
No Job, no prospects. His girl had left him 'cause he had no direction, no motivation and was friends with some right bad un's.

Action

    Dave interrupts

{Dave]:

What's your problem mate who are you ? The Narrator ?

[Narrator]:

Well yes, actually I am and you can't argue with me

[Dave]

Oh yes I can and I will

[Narrator];

Look Dave you are the master of your own destiney. I speak the truth when I tell you, you have no future.

Action

Dave Address' the audience
[Dave]:

I don't know why I wasn't good enough for Sue. Yeah I steal but I've never been caught, My brother is the bad one and that's not my fault. I've got good friends and they wont desert me.
I bloody loved that girl , still do, I ain't bad. **I've Done Her No Wrong !**

SONG SEVEN- DID YOU NO WRONG
Sex Pistols

I don't mind the things that you say
I don't even mind going out of my way
I try and do these things for you
Why should I do it
I'm always untrue

Well, I did you no wrong
I did you no wrong
Going out of your head

I ain't seen you off the screen
But those films are my dreams
And I can't take much more of you

'cause the bog is no place
To see your face

Can't you see I'm out of my head
Oh can't you see I'm a little insane
Oh can't you see I'm really dead

Going down, down, out of my head
I did you no wrong
I did you no wrong ! ha ha ha !

Going out of my head…

Action

Dave Clarke pacing up and down inside his bedroom. He is practising his explanation to Sue.

[Dave]: (Monologue)

See here Sue you've gotta listen to me. You've got to listen to me explain my feelings for you. I love you. I really love you. I would love it if you took me back. I know I'm not good but does that matter.

DAVE CLARKE CONTINUES TO PACE UP AND DOWN, HE STOPS AND BEGINS AGAIN.

[Dave]:

I love you Sue. All the things I've stolen and sold on the sly, its so I could buy things for you. Or take you places. Its all been for you.. can't you see that I love you ?

It like you have a strangle hold on me.

SONG EIGHT – STRANGLEHOLD
UK Subs

One two three
Four five six

Gotta do a dance
And it goes like this

Yeah some little girl's gotta hold on me
She's only thirteen but oh so sweet
Got me down on my knees
Got a stranglehold on me

Put's her arms around me like a vice
It's oh so painful but nice
But I can only take it once or twice
Got a stranglehold on me

Got a stranglehold on me
Got a stranglehold on me
Got a stranglehold on me
Stranglehold

Put's her arms around me like a vice
It's oh so painful but nice
But I can only take it once or twice
Got a stranglehold on me

Got a stranglehold on me
Got a stranglehold on me
Got a stranglehold on me
Stranglehold

Stranglehold on me
Stranglehold on me
Got a stranglehold on me
Stranglehold.

Five six seven
Eight nine ten
You want more?
We'll do it again

Stranglehold on me
Stranglehold on me

Stranglehold on me
Stranglehold.

[repeat several times]

Action

Mike Appears in the bedroom having been released from Borstal

[Dave]:

Hi Mick Just got out ?

[Mick]:

Yeah it was crap in there.
What's up with you ?

[Dave]:

My birds just dumped me

[Mick]:

Hahahah what a loser. Lets go for a pint, I got some mates for you to meet. .

End Of Scene Four

SCENE FIVE: PUB SCENE

Direction

Dave taken to the pub with Mick to meet some proper villains. The go to meet the Gang in pub. Mike greeted by members of a Firm

Cast Required
Dave
Dave' Dodgy Mates
Mick
Villains a Firm
Villain Gang member 1
Land Lord Pub
Pub Crowd
Police
Biker 1

Biker Girl

Action

Dave is taken by Mick to the pub to meet proper villains
Mick gets greeted by members of the Firm

[Mick]:

This is my little brother he's feeling a bit upset cos his bird has ditched him (laughs)

[Villain Gang member 1]:

"No worries, well sort you out mate".
Action

Dave meets and chooses to join the Firm.
During this next song the Gang intimidate patrons of the pub, They get up and leave.

SONG NINE: STARING AT THE RUDE BOYS
The Rutts

it's a very small world in the middle of a crowd
the room gets dark when the music gets loud
the rudies want to groove
but there's no room to move 'cause the floor is packed tight
a voice shouts loud
"we'll never surrender"
a voice in the crowd
"we'll never surrender"
a hand in the air fight propaganda
never surrender , never surrender
skins in the corner staring at the bar
the room starts dancing to some heavy heavy ska
the room is so hot people dripping with sweat
the punks in the corner , screaming like
staring at the rude boys
staring at the rude boys
dancing with the rude boys
dancing with the rude boys
staring at the rude boys
a bunch of skins , marching on ten
while some stand there saluting the air (oi!)
they wanna be pirates but the sea is not calm
tattooed crossbows on their arm's
the lights come alive in a blinding flash
the dance floor clears as the mutants clash
everybody leaves as the heavy's arrive
someone hits the floor, someone takes a dive

Action

Landlord confronts the villains.

[Landlord]:

"Settle Down lads otherwise I'm gonna call the police and have you thrown out".
Action

Villain Gang Members Glare at him
Mike is pleased Dave has joined the Firm and Dave loves the life style. As a celebration of Invincibility Dave stands on the table rejoicing.
Mod Dancing Northern Soul Style to **A Bomb.**

SONG TEN-A BOMB
The Jam

Where the streets are paved with blood,
With cataclysmic overtones,
Fear and hate linger in the air,
A strictly no-go deadly zone.
I don't know what I'm doing here
'cause it's not my scene at all
There's an 'A' bomb in Wardour Street
They've called in the Army, they've called in the police to.

I'm stranded on the vortex floor,
My head's been kicked in and blood's started to pour
Through the haze I can see my girl
15 geezers got her pinned to the door
I try to reach her but fall back to the floor
'A' bomb in Wardour Street
It's blown up the West End, now it's spreading throughout the City,

'A' bomb in Wardour Street, it's blown up the City
Now it's spreading through the country.

Law and order take a turn for the worst,

In the shape of a size 10 boot.
Rape and murder throughout the land,
And they tell you that you're still a free man.
If this is freedom I don't understand
'cause it seems like madness to me.
'A' bomb in Wardour Street, Hate Bomb,
Hate Bomb, Hate Bomb, Hate Bomb.

A Phillistine nation, of degradation,
And hate and war. There must be more
It's Doctor Martin's A,P,O,C,A,L,Y,P,S,E,
Apocalypse!

Action

After acceptance to villain gang Dave proposes a big fight to prove who's top dog.
[Dave]:

(Shouts) This is great !

[Villain Gang member 1]:

"Mick your brother's is well up for it".

[Dave]:
I'm bored let's go smash someone up!,

Action

The Gang are up for it. Dave Joins the band to sing.

<u>SONG ELEVEN –I'M AN UPSTART</u>
Angelic Upstarts

We don't need to be clever to learn your lies
We only have to listen, open up our eyes
Try to be honest, get kicked in the face
But if you cheat you're just a rat in the race

I'm an upstart
Hey whatcha gonna do

I'm an upstart
Listen I'm talking to you

Seek out an identity
You alienate society
Face the facts, why not admit it
How can you be outrageous when your mother won't allow it?
Action

Bikers arrive at pub and Dave confronts them

[Dave]:

"We don't want your sort in here" !
"Take your greasy filth elsewhere".

[Biker]:

"What did you say you cocky shit".

[Dave]:

You heard get out of here".

Action

Mick gets out a gun (A 22 Webley air pistol) and shoots a biker girl in the bum and laughs.
It all kicks off
Fight Scene to White Riot

[Biker Girl]:

"He shot me in the Arse ". (screaming)

SONG TWELVE-WHITE RIOT
The Clash

White riot - I wanna riot
White riot - a riot of my own
White riot - I wanna riot
White riot - a riot of my own

Black people gotta lot a problems
But they don't mind throwing a brick
White people go to school
Where they teach you how to be thick

An' everybody's doing
Just what they're told to
An' nobody wants
To go to jail!

White riot - I wanna riot
White riot - a riot of my own
White riot - I wanna riot
White riot - a riot of my own

All the power's in the hands
Of people rich enough to buy it
While we walk the street
Too chicken to even try it
Everybody's doing
Just what they're told to
Nobody wants
To go to jail!

White riot - I wanna riot
White riot - a riot of my own
White riot - I wanna riot
White riot - a riot of my own

Are you taking over
or are you taking orders?
Are you going backwards

Or are you going forwards?
Action

Police Arrive and make multiple arrests.

[Narrator]:

"Its all kicked off now. Dave and Mick have both been arrested for Drunken and disorderly conduct, malicious wounding and carrying a fire arm without a license .

Dave   Look Mike if you get done again you're down for serious time. I don't have any real form so if I tell the coppers it was me that shot the girl I will get off with probation. If you get done you will be recalled to Borstal or Prison.

Mike   Yes Ok that a good plan we will stick with that story.

[Narrator]:
At the court hearing Mike denied all charges but Dave, through miss guided loyalty copped to everything. Even the stuff he did 'nt do.... just to save his brother.
But the court saw through the lies and just found them both guilty.
Mick was sent to Maidstone Prison to join one of the Kray brothers and Dave to Dover Borstal an old haunt of Rod Stewart.
We are now going for a short break. See you back in 20 minutes".

End Of Scene Five

ACT TWO

47

SCENE SIX: PRISON CELL AT DOVER BORSTAL

Direction

Dave in cell in the prison cell.
The Devil Introduces herself to him and they both dance to (The Wait)

God introduces Himself. God a nice guy, Proper Hippy lovely nice bloke white suit sandals

Cast Required

Dave
Devil
God
Narrator

Action

Narrator says

[Narrator]:

"We resume our story with Dave banged up at HMP Dover Borstal Dave in his cell is deliberating on how he got into this mess."

Action

Devil comes on stage to The Wait.

SONG THIRTEEN: THE WAIT
Killing Joke

[One, two, three, four]

Motives changing, day to day
The fire increases, masks decay
I look at the river, white foam floats down
The body's poisoned, gotta sit tight

The wait
The wait
The wait
The wait
After wakening, silence grows
The screams subside, distortion shows
Mutant thoughts, of bad mouthed news
It's just another birth, of distorted views
The wait
The wait
The wait
The wait
The wait
The wait
The wait
The wait

Direction

[Devil]:

So Dave I suppose your wondering what you're doing here ?

[Dave]:

Well yeah this is no fun. I'm banged up and being banged up is boring as shit.

[Devil]:

Now , now Dave calm down you now have a golden opportunity here.

[Dave]:

What ?

[Devil]:

This is you chance to become a scholar in this fine establishment. At your disposal is all the talent you need to fulfil your destiny.
I can help your realise your every dream.

[Dave]:

"What do you mean?"

[Devil]:

50

Take this opportunity to get trained up by your fellow inmates, they are your new masters

Its time to get busy and plan your next move. You've got time to think things through and be more successful in your passion for the buzz of criminal behaviour.

[Dave]:

Slip out in the scrubs was a dirty task and all I did at Canterbury was four stitched to the inch sewing mail bags. You Mean Burglary, extortion, Drug deals, Protection, Pimping, Gambling, Fructuary, Ringing Cars and Kyte flying

You know your right I've made some foolish mistakes but never again. Next time I won't get caught.

[Devil]:

"That's my Boy" (cuddles him)

Action

God enters the cell

[God]:

Hang on Dave, don't listen to her. You're feeling depressed for a reason…

[Dave]:

What's that then...?

[God]:

You sinned and that's making you depressed.

[Dave]:

No I caught and that is making me feel sad.

[God]:

Well don't you think it's time to change...?

[Dave]:

Not really, I only just got started. Yeah I got caught but that's just bad luck. I'll learn some more stuff and then I'll be doing great!

[God]:

Well I see you all sad and depressed and I couldn't be you...

<u>SONG FOURTEEN-I COULDN'T BE YOU</u>
UK Subs

First of all they come along and say "there, put your baby in school"
But I was taught to win this game you must obey each golden rule
I said that I'm too young to die and can I wear my cowboy hat?
They said "wait a minute son, now that's the end of that"

And I couldn't be you if you wanted me to
And you couldn't be me if I begged you to be

They said that you're a big boy now, it's time to set you free in the world
Don't forget that steady job, and don't forget that steady girl
They said you start at nine o'clock and then we let you out at five
And if you act very smart you get a pension when you're 65

> I said I couldn't be you if you wanted me to
> And you couldn't be me if I begged you to be
>
> Said I couldn't be you if you wanted me to
> And you couldn't be me if I begged you to be

Action

Direction Devil Seduces God
Devil speaks to God

[Devil]:

What are you on about ?

"Dave is mine He is a fine student everything is going splendidly

[God]:

Dave is not yours he's mine

[Dave]:

Well we'll see (as she sexually taunts Dave. Dave laps it up.

[God]:

Now hang on Dave shes playing you.

[Dave]:

So This great please do carry on.
Action

Devil Address's God
[Devil]:

What's up, You created everything including me that's says to me that you want me too.

[God]:

Damn you

[Devil]:

You already did that.
Action

She seduces God and leaves him worn out on the bed. Dave looks on in delight.

SONG FIFTEEN-NICE AND SLEAZY
Stranglers

We came across the west sea
We didn't have much idea
Of the kind of climate waiting
We used our hands for guidance
Like the children of a preacher
Like a dry tree seeking water
Or a daughter
Nice'n'sleazy
Nice'n'sleazy does it
Nice'n'sleazy
Nice'n'sleazy
Does it does it every time
Nice'n'sleazy
Nice'n'sleazy
Does it does it every time
Nice'n'sleazy does it
Nice'n'sleazy
Nice'n'sleazy
Does it does it every time
Nice'n'sleazy does it
An angel came from outside
Had no halo had no father
With a coat of many colours
He spoke of brothers many
Wine and women song a plenty

He began to write a chapter In history
Nice'n'sleazy
Nice'n'sleazy does it
Nice'n'sleazy does it
Nice'n'sleazy does it
Does it every time

Action

God's angels rescue him from the devil she is too powerful he is escorted from the stage.
Dave tries to get in on the action with the Devil.

[Dave]:

"Come on baby lets have some"

[Devil]:

"You are not worthy for me yet you've got a lot to learn".

[Dave]:

"Don't you worry I will, I'll be your best student.... the law may have won this time

Action

Dave joins the band to sing I Fought the Law.

SONG SIXTEEN- I FOUGHT THE LAW
The Clash

Breakin' rocks in the hot sun
I fought the law and the law won (twice)
I needed money 'cause I had none
I fought the law and the law won (twice)
I left my baby and it feels so bad
Guess my race is run
She's the best girl that I ever had
I fought the law and the law won
I fought the law and the law won.

Robbin' people with a six-gun
I fought the law and the law won (twice)
I miss my baby and I miss my fun,
I fought the law and the law won (twice)

I miss my baby and I feel so sad
I guess my race is run
She's the best girl that I ever had
I fought the law and the law won (9 times)

[Narrator]:

Dave decides to get educated in Borstal and becomes a true Borstal Graduate. He fought the Law and it had won this time but never again.

Dave used his time wisely. He has learnt well. Equipped with his newly attained Borstal scholarship at Her Majesties pleasure he has decided that life is going to be ruthless in the pursuit of happiness. No more little dodgy risks its time for the crime of the century !

We now catch up with Dave on his release from Borstal in the pub in his home town.

End Of Scene Six

SCENE SEVEN: PRISON RELEASE

Direction

Dave is released from Borstal dressed in his de-mob suite provided by the Government. He immediatley changes into is own cloths as he was embarrased to wear the Government suit of cloths given him by the Government. This demostrates he has no change of heart, some thing his Borstal training could not give him.

Cast Required
Dave
Villain Firm
Dave's Dodgy Mates
Drug Dealer

[Dave]:
I don't like these cloths I look like a right gimp.
I can't be seen dressed like this. I know what I an going to do !

Direction

He changes cloths and dumps his de mob suit in the bin.
Then he and goes to the pub to celebrate and meet up with every one and demonstrates he was now worst than he was when he was sent away.

Meeting The Crew

[Dave]:

Alright lads. Now I'm back out of Borstal and I got me my education I reckon its time to get started again.

[1 x Dave's Mates]:

How was prison, mate?

[Dave]:

Brilliant. I learnt so much, I have big, big plans for us.
But first I need a decent car and I have a plan how to get one.

Dave Mate 1   Go on then tell us the plan.

Dave   I have seen a lovely blue , G reg, Mini, in Hemel Hempteac. Is always parked there outside the railway station. I recone they catch a train to work and leave the car there all day. So if it goes missing in the morning, namely we borrow it, that won't know its gone until they come home. By that time it will be tuched up in bed and We are going to change number platess, respray it, and hey press to I have a new car.

Dave Mat 3   Well I'm up for it I will give you a hand. Got any other planes.

We're going to be the biggest gang around town. We'll run all the drugs and this town will belong to us. Protection, Fencing , extortion, Pimping every thing where their is money to be made. LOL. Now give me some drugs.

Action

Dave scores some drugs in pub from a crazy dealer friend.
None prescription drugs are delivered by a crazy drug dealer dressed in a white coat.

[Mate 1]:

Is that the Fast Non Prescription illegal Drug Delivery Service.
Great, please deliver a nice selection to The Good Intent.

Action: Crazy drug dealer dressed in a white coat arrives on a moped to deliver the drugs

[Dealer]:

Here you go Dave what do you want?

[Dave]:

"Surprise me!"

Action

Pissed up Dave and Mates his mates go back to Dave place for a smoke.
[Dave]:

"Come on you lot lets go back to my place and get wrecked"

SONG SEVENTEEN -READY STEADY GO
Generation X

Ready, Steady Go
I'm not in love with television
I'm not in love with the radio
I'm not in love with the Kings Road
Because I'm in love with Cathy McGowan – she said
Ready steady go – all things she said
Ready steady go – wasn't it fabulous
Ready (ready) steady (steady) go

I'm not in love with Juke Box Jury
I'm not in love with thank you Lucky stars
I'm not in love with TTTTwiggy
Because I'm in love with Cathy McGowan –she said
Ready steady go – all things she said
Ready steady go – wasn't it fabulous
Ready (ready) steady (steady) go
I'm still in love with the Beatles

I was in love with the Stones, no satisfaction
I was in love with Bobby Dylan
Because I'm in love with Rock'n'Roll

Ready steady go – all things she said
Ready steady go – wasn't it fabulous
Ready (ready) steady (steady) go
Ready steady go!
Go! Go! Go!
Ready steady go!
Ready steady Who
Ready steady Stone
Go! Go Go Go.

End Of Scene Seven

SCENE EIGHT: BEDROOM

Direction
Dave is sat on his bed happy getting stoned with his mates
The Devil appears and they both get stoned. Dave chucks his mates out
The devil is still up for it and amuses herself with his carcass

Cast

Aliens
Devil
Dave
Dave's Mates
Narrator
[Narrator]:

Ladies and Gentleman! May I present Dave Clarke the villain of Aylesbury! Three years of tyranny and crime have passed since we last walked beside our Dave Clarke! He's an expert in coercion now.
 Mike after serving 18 months of his sentence escaped from prison during which time he and Dave got into serious crime.
 Then Mike however got a girl fried, who kept him on the stright and narrow. He got a job but was finally arrested whilst working on a building site and was went back to Maidstone Prison to serve his full time.
 And now Dave lately is spending more and more of his time getting smashed off his face on drugs in his bedroom feeling pretty vacant.

Action

Dave and mates at flat getting wrecked to the song Pretty Vacant.

SONG EIGHTEEN- PRETTY VACANT
Sex Pistols

There's no point in asking
You'll get no reply
Oh just remember a don't decide
I got no reason it's all too much
You'll always find us out to lunch
Oh we're so pretty
Oh so pretty we're vacant
Oh we're so pretty
Oh so pretty
A vacant
Don't ask us to attend
'cos we're not all there
Oh don't pretend 'cos I don't care
I don't believe illusions
'cos too much is real
So stop your cheap comment
'cos we know what we feel
Oh we're so pretty
Oh so pretty we're vacant
Oh we're so pretty
Oh so pretty we're vacant
Ah but now and we don't care

There's no point in asking
You'll get no reply
Oh just remember a don't decide
I got no reason it's all too much
You'll always find me out to lunch
We're out to lunch.

62
Action
Devil comes around for a visit.

[Devil]:

Hi Dave what a fine specimen you've turned out to be (smiles)

[Dave]:

Hello Sweetheart long time no see. Fancy a smoke.

[Devil]:

Yeah..... try some of mine
[Dave]:

Think you boys had better disappear
Action

Mates leave thinking Dave is going to get his end away
Devil has a smoke with Dave
Dave crashes out. Devil plays with his carcass in disgust.

[Devil]:

Wake up Dave

Wake Up

Action
   Dave stirs
[Devil]:

Take some of this to wake you up

[Dave]:

What is it

[Devil]:

Just a bit of acid
Action

   Dave takes a tab and has the horrors to Captain Kirk aliens wander about the stage

SONG NINETEEN- CAPTAIN KIRK
Spizzenergi

I was beamed aboard the stars hip Enterprise
What I felt what I saw was a total surprise
I looked around and wondered can this be
Or is this the start of my insanity

Oh but it's true
As we went warp factor 2

And I met all of the crew
Where's Captain Kirk
I went to the bridge and we were tossed aboutIn the storm of the vortex
I was hit with a doubt
I saw in a dream in a memory of mine
Was it you was it me who was in all the time

Spock pulled me through
As we went warp factor 2
And someone I saw I knew
Who's Captain Kirk

So when I awoke from the dangers of space
I looked and I saw a familiar face
The time warp in space made a change in me
For I was the captain and the captain was me

Yes it's so true
As we went warp factor 2
The changes I had been through
As Captain Kirk
I'm Captain Kirk

Action

During the song Dave cries out to God for help
God appears and helps out Dave.

[Dave]:

Jesus help me
Jesus help me
Jesus help me
Jesus help me

[God]: to Dave

I'm here Dave You've been searching for a long time
[Dave]:

Please help me I'm going out of my mind on acid.

[God]:

What you've been going though it nothing compared to what hell is like

[Devil]:

Dave what's up ? Go with it just relax babe

[Dave]:

Leave me alone I can't handle you

[God]: to Devil

Leave him alone he's had enough of you

[Devil]: to God

He'll be back with me he cant resist me !

Action

Gods Angels console Dave on his bed.

[God]:

"Satan, Be Gone"
Action
Devil leaves

[Dave]

Thank you Lord. Thank you for saving me ... how can I ever repay you.

[Narrator]:

Dave knew he had to change his ways and wanted too.
He learned to read to find out who Jesus was.
Dave had been rescued. His life and loves have been catastrophic. He

was now on a mission to set things right with the help of new friends. Part of this was to face his Dyslexia and Manic Depression (that he was later diagnosed with). This enabled him to educate himself in a profession that would enable others to achieve their greater goals.

Empowered by understanding and empathy, Dave grew stronger in his resolve. He battles with Dyslexia to this day but despite this he went on to gain a Cert. Ed. Awarded by Birmingham University and taught as a lecturer in Electronics for over 20 years.

He also joined the Bierton Strict and Particular Baptist church after 6 years and in 1982, he was ordained as a minister and taught the gospel of Christ. However the old guard could not cope with Dave's anarchistic approach.

He taught that any person can study and interpret the scriptures for themselves to their own satisfaction.

As part of his own reformation he confessed to the police about all his outstanding crimes. The police and Aylesbury Magistrates were only too happy to oblige.

But all that is in the future let's get back to the past for the past is another county and they do things differently there.

We now catch up with Dave at Aylesbury Magistrate court 9th February 1971 representing himself to answer the self confessed criminal charges.

End Of Scene Eight

SCENE NINE: COURT ROOM

Direction

Dave now dresses in a modest suit of cloths in order to appear in court. Dave stands before the magistrate in his modest from of dress and tells his story. This new dress symbolised his inner change of heart. He was a new man with a new heart and now his cloths reflected this.

Dave Admits to the charges that he has been brought to court for.

POLICEMEN are around DAVID CLARKE as he is stood in the dock. The MAGISTRATES are present, flanked by GOD and the DEVIL. Dave's gang are in the public gallery

Cast Required

Dave
Copper 1
Copper 2
Dave's Dodgy Mates
God
Devil
Magistrate third
Clerk to the Court
Press
Court Crowd
Extra's

[Clerk to the Court]:

Order in the Court

Mr Clarke would you please stand up. You have been brought before this court to answer the alleged crimes

Action

Dave Stands Up

Dave interrupts

[Dave]:

No they're not alleged.

Action

Gallery laughs

[Dave's Mates]:

(Mates cheer him on) "Go on Dave".

[Clerk to the Court]:

Order in the Court !

[Dave]:

Now let me explain why I am here. You have before you a list of all my crimes. I am not doing this as part of a plea. I was high most of the time and petty crime was my life. I had a bad trip on LSD and faced the horrors. I called out to God for help saying Jesus please elp me. God came to save me from myself. Its through his influence that I am here to take responsibility and to square my lot with everyone and society.

[Magistrate]:

Are you on drugs now Mr Clarke ?

[Dave]:

No you aren't listening, you don't understand, there is more to this...this is not just something that I am saying...

Action

From Gallery Mates cheer him on

Clerk to the Court

Silence in Court

[Dave]:

Your honour I stand before you please allow me to confess to my crimes I renounce may past life and the behaviour of any accomplices who may or may not have been there.

Action

More cheering from Gallery interrupts Dave's speech.

[Dave]: continues

"Your Honour I apologise for my crimes . I am a changed man and I apologise for them" (pointing at the gallery)

Action

Noise from the gallery.
Dave's mates can't take it they get more agitated.
Dave turns to the gallery.

[Dave]:

Sorry lads but you are part of my past life, I'd appreciate it if you would take this seriously.

[Dave's mates]

booh !

[Dave]:

Was it Something That I Said ?

Action

As the song plays Dave's mates get up and leave in disgust.

SONG TWENTY- SOMETHING THAT I SAID
The Rutts

OK, kick me in the head
Just cause something that I said
You don't want to know the truth
Cause you're wild and full of youth

Was it something that I said
Something that I said
Something in my head?

You ain't got no friends no more
Cause you kicked them to the floor
Time will tell, and you will see
That it's down to you, not me

Was it something that I said
Something that I said
Something in my head?

OK, now you're on your own
Your self-righteousness has grown
So get off your pedestal
Before you ain't got no friends no more

Was it something that I said
Something that I said
Something in my head?

[Dave]: Deliberates ??

You see I am confessing. I have a confession to make. I want to admit my crimes and start with a fresh slate.

I FEEL I'VE DONE IT, BROKEN OUT OF MY OWN BORSTAL STATE OF MIND

SONG 21 -BORSTAL BREAKOUT
Sham 69

I'm sitting in this cell for something I didn't do
And all I can think of is baby I think of you
Don't worry baby coming back for you
There's gonna be a Borstal Breakout

There's gonna be a Borstal Breakout
There's gonna be a Borstal Breakout
There's gonna be a Borstal Breakout

Now I've got the chance I don't care about what I do
When I done them things I done them just for you
And now I'm getting out coming back for you

There's gonna be a Borstal Breakout
There's gonna be a Borstal Breakout
There's gonna be a Borstal Breakout
There's gonna be a Borstal Breakout
Well now I'm over the wall I'm nearly home
I'm coming through that door back to you
Now I'm nearly home nearly back for you

There's gonna be a Borstal Breakout.

Direction
Court Bestows Sentence

[Chairman of the Magistrate]:

You have pleaded guilty to many crimes.
Your crimes have been the worst we have ever seen. We have considered what we aught to do and we have come to the conclusion your evident desire to become a martyr is one we are not going to gratify your are conditionally

discharged for a period of three years.

[Dave]:

Your Honour do you mean I am free to go ?

[Chairman of the Magistrate]:

Yes Mr Clarke please leave now and be quick about it before we change our minds we don't want to see you again

[Narrator]:

Its a miracle !! How did this happen virtually getting off scot free. Unbelievable but true. Dave and his new found friends leave the court and go to the pub to celebrate.

End Of Scene Nine

SCENE TEN: PUB

Direction

Dave and his new friends , including the Devil and God, go to the pub to celebrate
Dave deliberates about loosing his friends
Dave questions God and the Devil
Dave's old mates and villains turn up in the pub
Ends up in scuffle in a jealous rage against Dave and his new friends
God steps in. God stops the villian leader of the bad lads.
Landlord calls the police
Police arrive heavy handed and end up provoking a riot
Both groups of people end up against the police
All join in a the Dance

Cast Required

God
Devil
Dave
Narrator
Dave's New friends
Landlord
Dave Mates
Villain Firm
Action

Dave's news friends and others including the devil and God go to the pub to celebrate.

In the pub Dave says to God,

[Dave]:

Did you have something to do with that ?

Action

God smiles and gestures

[Devil to Dave]:

Well Dave happy with that ? (Smiling)

[Dave]:

Did you get me off that ? Did ya ?

Action

Devil (smiles and gestures)

[Narrator]:

Dave is confused. His old friends have abandoned him. His new friends celebrate with him. How did this happen. Was it the work of good or Evil

Has he taken the right path ? Is he invincible ? Does this mean he can always get away with anything ?

Dave has a choice to Stay or Go unlike his brother, who by the way died eventually in New Bilibid Prison, in the Philippines, of Tuberculosis, he had no choice.

SONG 22 - SHOULD I STAY OR SHOULD I GO
The Clash

Oh yeeeeeeaaaaaaah Wooh!
Darling you got
To let me know

Should I stay or should I go?

If you say that you are mine
I'll be here till the end of time
So you got to let me know
Should I stay or should I go?
Always tease, tease, tease
You're happy when I'm on my knees
One day is fine, next day is black
So if you want me off your back
Well come on let me know
Should I stay or should I go?

Should I stay or should I go now?
Should I stay or should I go now?
If I go there will be trouble
An' if I stay there will be double
So come on and let me know!
Should I stay or should I go ?

[Narrator]:

We are almost at the end of our punk rock opera , the story of David Clarke and his journey from bad to good.

Dave has completely changed and turned his life around. He has new goals, news friends, and now new direction. There may be trouble but for now he is feeling alright with his new crew.

SONG 23 -FEELIN' ALRIGHT WITH THE CREW
999

Time out the boys are rarin' to go
Tonight it's gonna be a hell of a show
You think you've got something to prove
Just wait and see who makes the first move
Your boots fit the occasion tonight
Tank up everything's going just right
Feelin' alright with the crew
Feelin' alright with the crew
Feelin' alright with the crew

Feelin' alright with the crew
I've got blood in my hair
And I want to smash you in the face so
What's the point in all this blood and confusion
Don't blink why this stupid battle
A curse it aggravates the metal
Outburst aint it ever going to settle down next time
I'm gonna even the score
You find that they'll be back for more

Feelin' alright with the crew
Feelin' alright with the crew
Feelin' alright with the crew
Feelin' alright with the crew

SCENE ELEVEN: PUB SCENE Continued

Action

Dave 's Mates and Villain Firm comes into the pub and taunt Dave.

[Villain Firm gang member 1]:

Hey Dave who are your new friends. Are we not good enough for you ?

[Dave}:

Hi come and join us

[Villain Firm gang member 1]:

You must be joking I wanta know if you have grassed me up (and moves forward to hit Dave)

[Dave]:

No mate ! of course not. You know there is honour amongst thieves. That still stands.

Action

God steps in.
[God]:

Just a moment (as he stops the Villain Firm member doing damage)

Action

Everyone Kicks Off.
Landlord steps in to call to the trouble and has to call then police.

Police arrive heavy handed at the Pub. Siren going in the back ground.

[Landlord]:

Right lads stop the grievance or I'll call the police and get you kicked out.
[Villains mates]:
Keep out of this you old goat

[Landlord]:

Police please they have kicked of in my pub

Action

Police arrive with sirens going and enter the pub.

[Police 1]:
All against the wall !!

Action

All gangs and everyone including the Devil and God, react against the police for interfering .

Eventually ALL CHARACTERS are dancing by the end of 'POLICE AND THIEVES'. Everyone is enjoying the music and have mutual respect for on another. They sing and rock out and dance to Police And Thieves.

[Narrator]
It might be hard for you to imagine, but its true. Our Dave Clarke here is going to be a good man. A teacher and lecturer. Helping otherto reach their full potential. But this is a Punk Rock Opera, and its time for one final big throw down. Just the MOD's and the ROCKER'S and DAVE'S MATE's. The Fowler Mean and DAVE's OLD DODGY MATES.

<u>SONG 24 POLICE AND THIEVES</u>
The Clash

Police and thieves in the streets
Oh yeah!
Scaring the nation with their guns and ammunition
Police and thieves in the street
Oh yeah!
Fighting the nation with their guns and ammunition

From Genesis to Revelation
The next generation will hear me
From Genesis to Revelation
The next generation will hear me

And all the crowd comes in day by day
No one stop it in anyway
And all the peacemaker turn war officer
Hear what I say

Police, Police, police and thieves oh yeah
Police, police, police and thieves oh yeah

From Genesis oh yeah
Police, police, police and thieves oh yeah
Scaring, fighting the nation
Shooting, shooting their guns and ammunition

Police, police, police and thieves oh yeah
Police, police, police and thieves oh yeah

Here come, here come, here come
The station is bombed
Get out get out you people
If you don't wanna get blown up

THE SECOND FIGHT HAS NEUTRALIZED ITSELF WITH THE RETURN OF THE POLICE
ALL THE RIVAL FACTIONS JOIN UP AGAINST THE POLICE,
FIGHT THE SYSTEM

[Narrator Summation and Conclusion]:

Dave went on to study and do well, he is happy and good to those around him. Dave met someone new who pushed him on to greater things. Now while Dave did all fancy stuff book learning to supplement his life learning, his brother went back to jail.

Mick Clarke's tale ends abroad in a prison, where we are sad to report. Mick died of tuberculosis but not before they two worked together helping other prison inmates in their reformation and rehabilitation.

Now we know why our Dave Clarke is the hero of the piece. He is a man who changed direction for good and went on to do well.

The very existence of this production is a testimony to Dave's ambition to allow the innocent and guilty to expand their minds and ability for the better in a true punk fashion to just do it your self.

And now before we get too slushy, here are our musical masterminds of mayhem to play us out

SONG 25 MR VERY GUILTY
Borstal Boys

1 Taken to the court house, by the powers that be.
In answer to the charges, had to make a plea.

Mr very guilty took them by surprise.
Having no defense set forth my demise.

Very, very guilty there is no other plea.
Yes very, very guilty looks like 3 years for me.

2 Made up my portfolio, listing all my crimes,
and knew with my past history, I was doing time.

Told the court my teenage past, and as I addressed the bench,
there, was my silver girl a love that made no sense

Very, very guilty there is no other plea.
Yes very, very guilty looks like 3 years for me.

3 She was now a magistrate , how would all this end.
Once she was my sweetheart, loved her to the end.

That Dear John that she give me , sent me round the bend,
Off into the night I drove, my life was at an end.

Very, very guilty there is no other plea.
Yes very, very guilty looks like 3 year to me.

4 Far more to my story, and was intent to tell.
Stood before the court that day, told of my trip to hell.

Told them all in detail, about my life of crime
since leaving Dover Borstal, 1969.

Very, very guilty there is no other plea.
Yes very, very guilty looks like 3 year to me.

Riff

Very, very guilty there is no other plea.
Yes very, very guilty looks like 3 years to me

Band Original
Borstal Boys Original
Every body dances to the end

THE END

FURTHER PUBLICATIONS

CONVERTED ON LSD TRIP

By David Clarke (Author)
3rd Edition Paperback – 3 Jun. 2020

This third edition of, 'Converted on LSD Trip', is written to bring attention to the reality of the work of the Lord Jesus Christ, in changing the lives of David Clarke, whilst on a bad trip on LSD, on 16th January 1970, and the life of his brother Michael Clarke, some 30 years later, when a prisoner, in the Philippines, and making them evangelist workers seeking to teach the gospel of Christ to men. It is intended to use this book as a tool for evangelism in order to encourage others in the work of preaching the gospel of Christ to men. This is also intended to draw attention to the work of Jesus Christ now in Baguio City, Philippines , by William O. Poloc a former inmate of New Bilibid Prison. It is believed and stressed that it is important to teach the traditional Christian doctrines of grace, to combat the error of modern-day Godliness, unbelief, homosexuality, feminism, Islam and of the importance of teaching the Deity of the Lord Jesus Christ, and the infallibility of the word of God

View as a video book (click to view)

BORSTAL BOYS

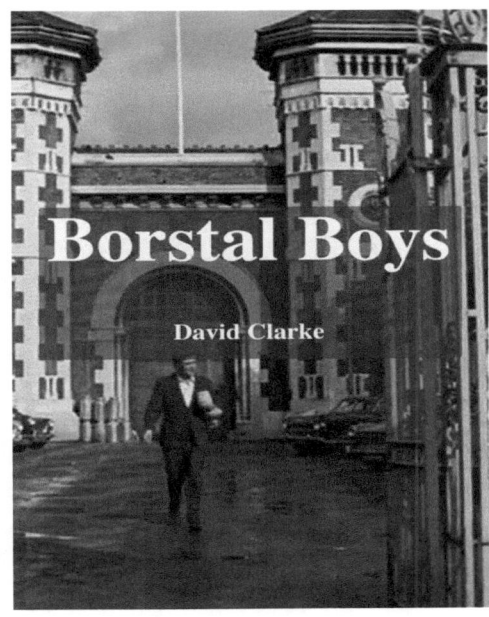

This is a true story of redemption, first told in the author's book, Converted on LSD trip, Bierton Strict and Particular Baptists, and From Crime To Christ.

Borstal Training was intended to reform seriously delinquent young people in the United Kingdom and the Commonwealth. It was devised in 1895. In India, Borstal was known as a Borstal School. The Gladstone Committee (1895) first proposed the concept of the Borstal, wishing to separate youths from older convicts in adult prisons. It was the task of Sir Evelyn Ruggles-Brise, a prison commissioner, to introduce the system, and the first such institution was established at Borstal Prison in a village called Borstal, near Rochester, Kent, England in 1902.

The system was developed on a national basis and formalised in the Prevention of Crime Act 1908. The regimen in these institutions was designed to be "educational rather than punitive", but it was highly regulated, with a focus on routine, discipline and authority during the early years, though one commentator has claimed that "more often than not they were breeding grounds for bullies and psychopaths." The Criminal Justice Act 1982 abolished the borstal system in the UK This book Borstal Boys tells the true story of two brothers who were sent to Borstal in the mid 1960's and clearly these were not reformed as this story will tell. However on the 16th January, 1970 David, the younger brother had a sudden conversion to Christianity, after a bad trip on LSD and turned his back on his criminal past. It was some 30 years later his brother Michael too, after serving 5 years of a 16 year sentence in the Philippines, became a Christian and he too turned his back on his criminal past. This book tells the whole story.

BORSTAL BOYS PUNK ROCK OPERA

1 YOUTUBE VIDEO
2 YOUTUBE VIDEO

This a musical that tells the true story of two brothers Michael and David Clarke, who were young criminals in the 60's. The story is told in full in Borstal Boys, by David Clarke.

David the younger found Redemption after a bad trip on LSD and turned his back on his criminal past on the 16th of January Jesus Christ spoke to him he learned to read to educate himself as at that time he was virtually illiterate and went on to higher education became a Baptist minister went on to higher education and taught electronics for over 20 years sadly Michael was unaffected by his brother's conversion to Christianity and died in prison of tuberculosis in the Philippines thirty-five years later this opera employs a live punk rock band performing 12 classic punk rock tracks telling the whole story the story's sole of the author's book converted on LSD trip now republished in the book the in Particular Baptists especially written for religious people

AND SUCH WERE SOME OF YOU

This story was first told in Converted on LSD Trip, by David Clarke but due to front cover and titles causing people to reject, even taking a look at the story has be reproduced with two different front covers.

AND SUCH WERE SOME OF YOU

This story was first told in Converted on LSD Trip, by David Clarke but due to front cover and titles causing people to reject, even taking a look at the story has be reproduced with two different front covers.

TROJAN WARRIORS

Setting Captives Free

Authored by Mr David Clarke CertEd, Authored by Mr Michael J Clarke

Trojan Warriors is a true story of two brothers, Michael and David Clarke, who are brought up in Aylesbury, Buckinghamshire, England. They became criminals in the 60's and were sent to prison for malicious wounding and carrying a fire arm without a license, in 1967.

They both turned from their lives of crimes in remarkable ways but some 25 years apart, and then they worked together helping other prison inmates, on their own roads of reformation.

David the younger brother became a Christian, after a bad experience on LSD, in 1970, and then went on to educate himself and then on to Higher Education. He became a baptist minister and taught electronics for over 20 years, in colleges of Higher and Further Education. Michael however remained untouched and continued his flamboyant life style ending up serving a 16 year prison sentence, in the Philippines, in 1996, where he died of tuberculosis in 2005.

When David heard the news of his brothers arrest on an ITN television news bulletin he felt compelled to wrote their story. And then when he heard of his own brothers conversion from crime to Christ, after serving 5 year of his sentence, he published their story in his book, "Converted on LS Trip", and directed a mission of help to the Philippines to assist his brother. This book tells the story of this mission.

They then worked together with many former notorious criminals, who were inmates in New Bilibid Prison, who too had become Christians and turned their lives around. This help was to train them to become preachers of the gospel of Jesus Christ .

This book contains the 66 testimonies of some of these men who convicted former criminals, incarcerated in New Bilibid Prison. They are the, "Trojan Warriors", who had turned their lives around and from crime to Christ. Twenty two of these testimonies are men who are on Death Row scheduled to be executed by lethal injection.

Revelation 12 verse 11: And they overcame him by the blood of the lamb and the word of their testimony and they loved not their lives unto the death.

BEFORE THE COCK CROWS PART 1, 2 AND 3.

| PART 1 | PART 2 | PART 3 |

By David Clarke

David Clarke the Director of Trojan Horse International CM encountered remarkable opposition from various quarters in New Bilibid Prison, Muntinlupa City Philippines between October 2002 and July 2003. Most of those who opposed the mission were men from among Asia's most notorious criminals in the National Penitentiary, which is situated on the Reservation at Muntinlupa City, 1770, Philippines. If one were to judge the success of the mission by that amount of opposition that it experienced, then the mission was a remarkable success. Newton stated that to every force there is an equal but opposite one to oppose it and like Newton, David suggests that to every proactive work there is and equal but opposite reaction and so if this reaction were to be the measure of success, then the mission was remarkably successful. It also serves to demonstrate that God always triumphs. That God saves, not by might, but by His Spirit. That God puts to fight thousands of his enemies and empowers the one's and two's, that trust in Him in order to show that Salvation is truly of the Lord. This prison comprises of three Compounds and penal farms housing over 23,550 inmates, which are all under the control of the Department of Justice (DOJ) and the Bureau of Corrections. (BUCOR). The Chaplaincy, headed by Msgr. Helley Barrido, is responsible for all religious groups and voluntary work done within the Prison. "Death Row" is in the Maximum Security Compound where over 1200 men are housed and they are all under the sentence of death. Some are doubly confirmed and due to be put to death by lethal injection. Trojan Horse International C.M. was established in the early part of 2001 and composed of a team of two from England, David Clarke and Gordon John Smith. The mission was set up as a Christian ministry, seeking to bring assistance to Michael John Clarke, David's older brother, and many inmates at the Prison. This was where Michael had been incarcerated, for a crime he did not commit, and was serving a prison sentence of 16 years. He had been baptized as a Christian. In an old 45-gallon US Oil drum, on the 16th September 2000 in the Maximum Compound. Michael, like his brother David, had been converted from crime to Christ whilst suffering the bitter effects of this form of injustice in the Philippines. How ever Michaels conversion was some thirty years after David who had been brought up in Aylesbury, Buckinghamshire and had been converted from crime to Christ, at the age of 20 years old, on the 16th January 1970.

THE FALL, DESPERATION AND RECOVERY

By Mr David Clarke CertEd (Author)

David encountered great conflicts of conscience whilst at the Bierton Strict and Particular Baptists Church and seceded over matters of conscience. For two years he wondered what the future held for him and wondered about the direction that he should go. This led him to severe depression thinking that God had rejected him and then to a desperate state of mind resulting in him turning away from God and to open sin. This is the continuing story of David life as told in his book , "Converted on LSD Trip", and relates the journey that led to his fall, the desperation, recovery and restoration to faith in Christ . He tells of the good news he received of his brother Michael and his conversion from crime to Christ, that took place 5 years into a 16 year prison sentence, in the Philippines. This was 30 years after David 's own conversion from crime to Christ, which was the moving factor behind publishing his book, "Converted on LSD Trip." David believes this book will be very useful for people of all ages who wish to see the hand of God at work and in particular for those learning the Christian faith.

L - #0197 - 141122 - C0 - 229/152/5 - PB - DID3421968